The Freedom Formula

How Letting Go Transforms Your Life and Unlocks True Happiness

Kenneth. M Rollins

Table of Contents

Introduction

In a society where we are continuously encouraged to take control, plan every detail, and mold our lives carefully, letting go may seem contradictory. Society teaches us that success comes from firmly gripping the reins, manipulating every scenario, and shaping the universe to match our expectations. However, for millions of individuals who have experienced the freeing power of letting go, a new reality is emerging: control is often an illusion and genuine pleasure comes from accepting uncertainty and abandoning the desire for control.

The Freedom Formula is founded on a simple but significant concept: by letting go of our urge to control people, manipulate events, and compel life to go our way, we make room for calm, development, and unexpected chances. This technique is not about giving up or being passive; rather, it is about learning to trust the natural flow of life and understanding that freedom is found not in controlling results, but in mastering how we react to them.

Why Letting Go Is Essential

Throughout our lives, we are taught that having more control means having a better life. We make plans, establish objectives, and create expectations. Although there is a benefit to being focused and proactive, we often forget that life is unexpected. Circumstances change, individuals adapt, and results often deviate from our initial expectations or goals. When we get too committed to a certain outcome, we set ourselves up for disappointment, anger, and even pain.

But what if there was another way to deal with life's twists and turns? The Freedom Formula enables you to appreciate the beauty of uncertainty. Letting go does not imply abandoning your aspirations or objectives; rather, it entails relinquishing control over how they are realized. It's about believing that life has its rhythm and that when we stop battling that flow, we discover a deeper, more enduring satisfaction.

Consider this: how many times have you spent sleepless nights worried about a relationship, a career, or a choice that seemed to be spiraling out of control? How much energy have you spent attempting to persuade someone to change, remedy a problem, or make your life fit a predefined mold? These conflicts are tiresome because they contradict the natural flow of existence. The greater we strive to exert control, the more we prevent ourselves from enjoying genuine pleasure and inner serenity.

The Path To Freedom

This book is not a call to give up ambition or effort. Instead, The Freedom Formula provides a new paradigm for living more freely and cheerfully in a world full of uncertainty. It reminds us that letting go is a sign of strength. It permits us to create room for acceptance, resilience, and adaptability—characteristics that allow us to flourish regardless of what life throws at us.

The power of letting go may be felt in many aspects of life, including relationships, employment, personal development, and the pursuit of aspirations. Imagine no longer attempting to control people's perceptions of you, no longer being crushed by rejection and dreading failure since you've learned to accept it as part of the process. Letting go does not imply that you cease caring; rather, it implies that you let go of the impulse to control the result and instead allow yourself to deal with whatever happens.

What You'll Learn in This Book

The Freedom Formula will help you navigate the significant mental and emotional changes that occur when you learn to let go. In the following pages, you will find the skills you need to break free from the restraints of perfectionism, control, and overthinking. You'll hear true tales of individuals who have changed their lives by letting go of what they couldn't control, allowing joy and opportunity to enter in unexpected ways.

Each chapter provides practical actions and ideas to help you apply the concepts of letting go of different elements of your life.

- Reclaim your emotional energy by letting go of the need to repair or control others.
- Strengthen your relationships by accepting people as they are, rather than how you believe they should be.
- Transform failure and rejection into tremendous development chances by disconnecting from bad consequences.
- Unlock real happiness by believing that life will develop in ways that are frequently better than you could have anticipated.

This path is about developing faith in yourself and the flow of life. It's about realizing that the freedom you want doesn't come from controlling everything around you, but from managing your inner world. Once you comprehend the power of letting go, you will discover that life becomes more enjoyable, relationships become more rewarding, and your potential for progress is infinite.

 A New Way of Living

Letting go is not a one-time occurrence; it is a mentality, a habit, and a lifestyle. It represents a transition from fearing uncertainty to accepting it as a source of possibilities. When you learn the Freedom Formula, you'll start to feel lighter, less burdened by life's stresses, and more receptive to the opportunities that come your way. You will get a greater feeling of calm and resilience, knowing that no matter what occurs, you are capable of adjusting and prospering.

As you read this book, you will be encouraged to consider areas in your life where you are holding on too firmly. You'll be asked to consider how your need for control may be limiting your happiness and inhibiting your progress. Most importantly, you'll be equipped with the means to embrace a new way of life—

one based on the freedom
that comes with letting go.
Welcome to the start of a
transformational adventure.
The road to real pleasure and
inner liberation begins with
the simple but profound
choice to let go.

Power of Letting Go

In a world that often pushes
us toward control, perfection,
and the pursuit of certainty,
the idea of letting go can feel
counterintuitive. Yet, letting go
is one of the most powerful
actions we can take to reclaim
our peace and emotional
freedom. At the heart of this
concept is the "Let Them"
theory—a simple but profound
mindset that encourages us to
release our grip on others'
actions, behaviors, and
decisions, thereby freeing
ourselves from the stress of
attempting to control the
uncontrollable. This shift in
mindset is transformative, as

it leads to greater inner peace, improved relationships, and emotional resilience.

Understanding the "Let Them" Theory

The "Let Them" theory is built on the principle of surrendering the need to control external factors, especially other people's behaviors and choices. It is based on the realization that we cannot change others, nor can we control how events unfold in life. Instead, the only thing we can control is our response. By consciously choosing to "let them" do as they will, we relinquish the emotional burden of trying to dictate or manipulate outcomes.

This does not mean that we stop caring or become passive bystanders in our lives. Rather, the "Let Them" theory empowers us to focus our energy on what truly matters: our well-being, growth, and responses to situations. It is a call to release the need for perfection, approval, or validation from others and to trust that we can thrive regardless of what others choose to do or how life plays out.

The Power of Releasing Control

One of the key benefits of adopting the "Let Them" mindset is the profound sense of emotional freedom it creates. Many of us carry an invisible weight—the weight of trying to manage others' expectations, behaviors, and opinions. This constant effort to control not only leads to frustration and disappointment but also drains our energy and peace of mind.

By letting go, we release the pressure to be responsible for others' happiness or success. We stop assuming that their actions are a reflection of our worth. Instead, we grant them the freedom to live as they choose, while granting ourselves the freedom to prioritize our own emotional well-being. This shift alleviates the anxiety of needing things to go a certain way and reduces the internal friction caused by unmet expectations.

Inner Peace Through Acceptance

At the core of the "Let Them" theory is acceptance— accepting people for who they are and situations for what they are, without trying to impose our will upon them. This acceptance does not mean we condone harmful behavior or resign ourselves to unfavorable circumstances. Instead, it means recognizing the limits of our influence and choosing to direct our energy toward what we can control: our thoughts, actions, and responses.

Inner peace comes from this place of acceptance. When we release the need to control, we stop resisting reality. We learn to navigate life with greater fluidity, responding rather than reacting. Whether someone fails to meet our expectations, a relationship changes, or life throws unexpected challenges our way, the "Let Them" mindset allows us to approach these moments with grace. Instead of feeling defeated by what we cannot change, we focus on our power to adapt and grow.

Letting Go and Personal Boundaries

An essential aspect of the "Let Them" theory is setting healthy personal boundaries. While we embrace the idea of letting go, we also maintain clarity about what is acceptable in our lives. Letting go does not mean tolerating toxic behavior or allowing others to overstep your boundaries. On the contrary, it is about recognizing that while we cannot control others, we do have the right to determine how we engage with them and what behaviors we will allow in our lives.

When we let go of the need to change others, we become more effective in setting and enforcing boundaries. We stop wasting energy on trying to make someone behave differently and instead focus on protecting our peace. This might mean distancing ourselves from harmful situations, speaking up when necessary, or simply walking away when a situation no longer serves our well-being.

The Emotional Freedom of Non-Attachment

Non-attachment is a key principle in many spiritual traditions, and the "Let Them" theory echoes this wisdom. Non-attachment means not clinging to specific outcomes, people, or situations for our sense of happiness. It is the understanding that while we can strive for goals and build relationships, we are not defined by these external factors. Our emotional freedom comes from within, from our ability to let go of the need to control and trust the flow of life.

By adopting non-attachment, we stop investing so much of

our emotional energy in how things "should" be. We begin to trust that things will unfold as they are meant to, even if the outcome is not what we originally envisioned. This detachment allows us to enjoy life's experiences without the fear of loss or disappointment, knowing that our inner peace is not dependent on external circumstances.

Transforming Relationships

The "Let Them" theory is particularly powerful when applied to relationships. Often, conflict and dissatisfaction in relationships arise from unmet expectations or the desire to change another person. We want others to behave in ways that align with our needs, values, or desires, and when they don't, it can lead to frustration and resentment.

By adopting a "let them" approach, we free ourselves from the unrealistic expectation that others should conform to our standards. We allow people to be who they are, without judgment or attempts to mold them into what we want them to be. This creates space for healthier, more authentic relationships, where mutual respect and acceptance thrive. We stop trying to change others and start appreciating them for who they are, flaws and all.

In turn, this mindset can also inspire change in others—not because we force it, but because our acceptance creates an environment where growth and self-improvement feel safe. When people feel accepted as they are, they are more likely to be open to change, growth, and vulnerability.

Practical Steps to Embrace the "Let Them" Mindset

1. Self-Awareness: Recognize the situations where you feel the urge to control. Reflect on why you feel the need to manage others' actions or outcomes.

2. Mindful Acceptance: Practice acceptance in your daily life. When faced with something beyond your control, remind yourself to let it go. Acknowledge your feelings, but consciously release the desire to force a specific outcome.

3. Focus on Your Response: Instead of trying to change others or the situation, focus on how you will respond. What action will serve your peace of mind and well-being?

4. Set Boundaries: Letting go doesn't mean you allow anything and everything. Define your boundaries and be clear about what is acceptable to you, then enforce them without trying to change others.

5. Trust the Process: Let go of the need to know or control what will happen next. Trust that life has a way of working out, even if it's not in the way you expected.

6. Detach from Outcomes: Practice non-attachment by

embracing the idea that you can strive for what you want, but your happiness doesn't depend on a particular result.

The power of letting go lies in the freedom it offers. When we stop trying to control others or outcomes, we reclaim our energy, peace, and emotional balance. The "Let Them" theory reminds us that our greatest power lies not in controlling the world around us but in controlling how we engage with it. Through acceptance, non-attachment, and mindful boundaries, we unlock the door to a more peaceful, resilient, and empowered life.

The Science Behind Letting Go

Whether it's quitting a job, breaking up with someone, or leaving a location, we've all had to master the tough skill of letting go.

Unfortunately, learning to let go is more difficult than

hanging on. Humans have a propensity to identify themselves based on what they possess, so we hold onto previous misfortunes, terrible relationships, and even pointless objectives.

We carry grudges, reflect on past errors, and assign emotional value to inanimate items. This is a lot to bear – a burden that might hamper your capacity to discover, create, and redefine yourself.

Fortunately, learning to let go is both scientific and artistic. Here are five easy activities you may do to lose some of this weight and start enjoying a lighter, freer life.

1. Let go of things.

Let us start with the most practical level of letting go. Mari Kondo developed a great company by assisting individuals in decluttering their houses by letting go of their outdated belongings. Why do individuals find it so difficult to let go of these tangible possessions?

Sometimes it's because they have sentimental worth. This emotive worth might be derived from previous experiences or future aspirations. Objects having prior emotional worth may be a keepsake from a vacation, a jewelry you wore on your first date, or a cup your grandma gave you.

Objects with potential emotional worth may include a box of craft tools for when you finally start learning how to paint, a collection of architectural books that you will undoubtedly read at some point, or a set of kettlebells for when you work at home – someday. Letting go of things feels similar to letting go of a dream.

Other times, we are afraid of being wasteful. Either we believe we will need that item again or we feel terrible about spending the money on it in the first place. The sunk cost fallacy has reared its ugly head.

A wonderful technique to get rid of clutter is to do it gradually. Begin with the simple stuff—things like devices you haven't used in years, old documents with no emotional value, or, the easiest of all, objects you don't even remember what they are or what they're meant to be used for. Most of us have a lot of them in our homes.

Gradually progress your decluttering efforts to more emotional objects, asking yourself "Why do I care about this item?"

Often, you will discover that the need that drives your emotional connection to a certain thing may be met in other ways, such as via a gratitude practice centered on the experience associated with the object or by writing about the memory in your journal.

This shouldn't be an uncomfortable procedure. Keep objects that you genuinely care about. Who cares how neat your house is? All that counts is that it feels like home.

2. Let go of ambitions.

Old ambitions are an unseen weight that we bear without realizing it. Although they may no longer reflect our present goals, they remain in our subconscious, affecting our choices and behaviors.

We sometimes cling to previous ambitions out of a false feeling of loyalty to our earlier selves. For example, you may feel forced to follow a job path that was established owing to familial expectations. Financial milestones, such as reaching a particular amount of money or acquiring property by a certain age, might place too much pressure on you.

The weight of outmoded aspirations might even emerge in areas that are often seen to be innately beneficial, such as wanting to run a marathon when your health may not allow it or seeking an advanced degree when your current circumstances make it impracticable.

In many circumstances, defined objectives might restrict your learning options. Some of the most intriguing discoveries we make are coincidental. Tinkering, playing, experimenting, and trying new things are all inherently gratifying hobbies that provide pleasure and intellectual stimulation without the requirement for a specific end objective.

Learning to let go of your objectives entails making time in your life to do things merely to do them, rather than because they fit neatly into a larger plan. Simply jot down your existing objectives and ask yourself, "Why should I care about this goal?"

Most objectives may be converted into long-term systems by focusing on the process rather than the outcome. If you want to learn, you don't have to set a precise goal. If you want recognition, show up regularly rather than sprinting to the finish line. If you want to feel useful, interact with people meaningfully rather than checking off checkboxes based on fake milestones.

3. Let go of control.

Everyone can tell when a boss micromanages their staff, when a coworker consistently takes the lead in discussions, or when a family member adheres to strict customs. It's more difficult to recognize our efforts to assert control over our surroundings. We may arrange every aspect of a trip without allowing for spontaneity or feedback from others. In our houses, we could prepare our meals ahead of time and have a regular cleaning routine. Or we may be so dedicated to our exercise program that we fail to take breaks when we are sick.

Recognizing these patterns in oneself is difficult because they often spring from a strong need for stability and predictability, making them seem more like required habits than controlling behaviors.

Most parents will also have an intense sense of having to let go of control: the terrible moment when they must let their child explore the world independently. It begins with their first step and only grows more difficult with time until they go to university or obtain their first job and move out of the home. Learning to let go of control may be exceedingly tough in this situation.

To break away from the illusion of control, we must first offer control before receiving control. In reality, this means allowing others (your child, your staff, and yourself) to bend the rules. It begins with asking oneself, "Why do I care about this rule?"

Then, rather than a set of inflexible rules like a psychological prison, create a playground with basic concepts that are flexible enough to allow for uncertainty and creativity. For example:

"You must finish all your homework before playing" (rigorous guideline) might become "Focus on finishing your tasks but remember to make time for fun too" (flexible principle).

"Exercise every day for exactly one hour" (rigorous rule) might become "Exercise three times a week, adjusting the intensity and duration to match your daily health and energy levels" (flexible concept).

"No sweets or junk food ever" (rigorous rule) might become "Focus on a balanced diet while allowing yourself the flexibility to enjoy treats in moderation" (flexible principle).

Finally, letting go of control will help you to embrace adaptation and flourish even when things don't go as planned.

4. Let go of people.

Let's turn it up a little. It may seem harsh, but it is

sometimes preferable to let go of some connections. Some connections may no longer represent your current self, or others may have matured in such a manner that the relationship has altered.

Learning to let go of a "legacy relationship" does not have to be a bad experience; it may be a chance for personal development. Ask yourself, "Why do I care about this relationship?"

A useful activity is to write a letter to the individual but not send it to them. Thank them for all you learned throughout the partnership. Allow yourself to feel the whole range of feelings that this practice may evoke, both pleasant and negative. Most of the relationships we care about are complicated. Accept that complexity.

Maintain a forgiving mindset during this practice. According to research, forgiving and wishing someone well may lead to greater health.

It's possible that going through this procedure may make you realize the connection is worthwhile. If that's not the case, gently let go, be thankful for the lessons you've learned about the world and yourself, and retain the positive memories as reminders of a relationship that has helped you develop.

5. Let go of the past.

We also have a tendency to hold onto memories, particularly those that are traumatic. That's because our brains are programmed to recall unpleasant events more vividly as a survival strategy, and these memories often have strong emotional connections that keep them alive in our minds. This is intended to assist us prevent such issues in the future.

However, this technique may occasionally backfire, causing us to continuously experience the unpleasant feelings connected with these memories, which can harm our emotional well-being and impede us from progressing.

Letting go of the past is difficult because it involves letting go of a part of ourselves. Our experiences shape who we are, and breaking free from the weight of old memories entails rebuilding our identity.

To begin this challenging but rewarding process, ask yourself, "Why do I care about this memory?"

To begin this challenging but rewarding process, ask yourself, "Why do I care about this memory?"

You may feel that recalling the anguish will avoid future harm.

You may regard this recollection to be an important part of your narrative.

You could have a deep emotional connection with the persons in this recollection.

You could be scared that forgetting would cause you to repeat the same errors.

Answering this question can help you replace static

memories with more generative ones. For example, you may keep a record of the major lessons learned from this memory and how you can prevent making a similar mistake in the future, or you could seek out more good events in your life that give healthier alternatives to reaffirm your identity.

In conclusion, here are the five questions you may use to practice the art and science of letting go.

Let go of things: "Why do I care about this item?"

Let go of goals: "Why do I care about this goal?"

Let go of control: "Why do I care about this rule?"

Let go of people: "Why do I care about this relationship?"

Let Go of the Past: "Why do I care about this memory?"

According to Eppie Lederer, "Some people believe that holding on and hanging in there are signs of great strength." However, there are moments when it requires much more power to know when to let go and then act."

Reclaiming Your Energy

In today's fast-paced, digitally connected society, many of us are always striving to influence outcomes, whether in our employment, personal relationships, or even our everyday routines. We attempt to ensure that everything goes as planned, frequently straining ourselves in the process. This need for control is emotionally taxing, leaving us irritated, nervous, and helpless when events stray from our expectations. The irony, of course, is that in our attempts to control everything, we often lose control of the most important thing: our emotional well-being.

This chapter delves into the transforming impact of regaining your energy by letting go of the impulse to control other people and situations. Adopting the Freedom Formula allows you to free up mental and emotional energies that are tied to results over which you have no control. Redirecting that energy toward personal development, creativity, and enjoyment allows you to live a more fulfilling and peaceful life.

 The Burden of Control

Much of our emotional tiredness stems from a deeply held idea that we must choreograph everything in our lives to succeed and be happy. This attitude may emerge in a variety of ways, including micromanaging duties at work, attempting to control how people act in relationships, and methodically arranging every aspect of our lives. We grow devoted to a certain idea of how things should be and devote enormous amounts of emotional energy to make that vision a reality.

However, life is fundamentally unpredictable. People have free choice, circumstances change, and unforeseen problems happen. When we cling to control, we often disrupt the natural flow of life. The continual push and pull to make things go our way causes tension, worry, and feelings of failure when things don't go as planned. It's as if we're swimming upstream, using more energy than required, just to get trapped in the same spot.

The Emotional Toll of Controlling Others

Attempting to manage others is one of the most tiring behaviors we may have. Whether it's attempting to persuade a spouse to modify their behavior, influencing a coworker's actions, or manipulating how friends and family react to us, this habit has a huge impact on our emotional well-being. We tend to associate our pleasure with the conduct of others, resulting in a loop of disappointment when individuals fail to match our expectations.

The fact is that everyone has their own path to take, and seeking to control others strains relationships while also robbing us of our own inner serenity. By blaming external sources for our pleasure, we give up our authority and become emotionally exhausted.

Accepting the Freedom Formula.

Enter the Freedom Formula, a liberating mentality change that has the potential to revolutionize our approach to control. The core of this idea is straightforward: Let them. Allow individuals to be who they are. Allow circumstances to develop as they will. Instead of attempting to control or influence results, accept that you cannot and should not have control over everything.

By letting go of the need to control individuals and events, you make room for acceptance and flow. When you let individuals be themselves without attempting to alter them, you will see that their decisions do not reflect you. You may still keep your limits and ideals, but remember that everyone is accountable for their actions and choices.

This approach is also applicable to life's uncertainty. Allowing circumstances to flow organically, rather than imposing a precise conclusion, relieves you of the emotional drain of continual concern and micromanagement. Instead of focussing on what you cannot control, you direct your attention to what you can control: your behaviors, thoughts, and how you react to the environment around you.

The Power of Reclaiming Your Energy

Reclaiming your energy by adopting the Freedom Formula entails more than simply giving up control; it also entails channeling that energy into more productive and rewarding activities. When you quit attempting to control others and results, you open up mental space that may be used for personal development, creativity, and enjoyment.

1. Personal Development

When you let go of the demand for control, you open yourself up to personal growth. The energy you used to devote to caring about others may now be used towards your self-improvement. You may invest in acquiring new skills, adopting healthier habits, or increasing your self-awareness. Personal development thrives when we concentrate on ourselves rather than attempting to alter others.

2. Creativity

Creativity flourishes when the mind is clear of anxiety and overthinking. By regaining your energy, you make mental room for new thoughts and inspiration to emerge. Whether it's painting, writing, problem-solving, or invention, creativity may thrive when we're not burdened by the emotional baggage of control. You may find yourself more willing to take chances, attempt new things, and pursue creative interests that you have previously overlooked.

3. Happiness

Happiness is a natural result of letting go of control. When we cease attempting to control everything and everyone around us, we relieve ourselves of the tension and anxiety that come with that responsibility. We learn to embrace life's unpredictability with grace, finding delight in the present moment rather than imagining a future in which everything happens as planned. Happiness occurs when we realize we don't have to manage the world to obtain inner peace.

Practical Steps for Reclaiming Your Energy

While the notion of letting go is straightforward, putting it into action may be difficult. Here are some practical strategies to help you regain energy:

1: Identify Control Patterns

Begin by recognizing areas where you are wasting energy attempting to control others or results. Are there any partnerships in which you attempt to control someone else's behavior? Are there areas of your life in which you are excessively concerned with controlling every detail? Awareness is the first step in breaking away from control tendencies.

2. Set boundaries, not expectations

It is critical to differentiate between establishing healthy limits and attempting to dominate people. Boundaries preserve your emotional and mental well-being, while control seeks to alter someone else. Focus on creating clear, healthy limits for yourself rather than attempting to manage the conduct of others.

3: Practice Acceptance

Acceptance is essential to recovering your vitality. Practice accepting people and events as they are, without attempting to impose your will. This does not imply that you condone bad behavior or just accept everything that occurs. Rather, it is about accepting that certain things are beyond your control and that your peace of mind does not rely on them.

4. Redirect your energy

When you see yourself drifting back into control habits, intentionally divert that energy. Instead of focusing on others, consider how you may channel that energy into your progress and enjoyment. Which aspects of your life need greater attention? How can you develop your creativity and follow your passions?

5. Trust the Process

Letting up of control requires faith in oneself, others, and the course of life. While it may seem unpleasant at first, believing that things will develop as they should helps you to let go of the need for control. Trust that you have the strength to deal with whatever comes your way and that life has a way of working out, even if it isn't exactly as you planned.

Reclaiming your energy means reclaiming your life. By letting go of the urge to control outcomes and others, you may lead a more tranquil, fulfilled, and joyous life. The Freedom Formula is an effective tool for shifting your perspective and focusing your energy on personal development, creativity, and pleasure. As you accept this transition, you'll notice that you have more energy, as well as a stronger feeling of freedom and power. After all, life is intended to be experienced rather than controlled.

Let Them Be Who They Are

The urge to modify or shape others is a frequent tendency, especially in interactions in which we have an emotional investment—whether in family, friendships, love engagements or even professional dynamics. However, learning to accept people for who they are without attempting to alter them is an important step towards developing better and more rewarding relationships. The problem is to strike a delicate balance between accepting and keeping personal limits.

The Trap of Expectations

Many marital problems stem from unreasonable expectations. We often get into the trap of expecting others to think, feel, or behave as we do, or as we believe they should. Whether it's a buddy who routinely makes terrible life decisions or a family member whose political opinions are diametrically opposed to yours, there's a natural want to "correct" them—to assume that by influencing their choices or perspectives, we're helping them develop or better.

However, this expectation causes stress. It presupposes control over another person, which we do not have. People are formed by their own experiences, traumas, cultural origins, and personalities. Attempting to modify them might elicit resistance, weaken trust, and eventually harm the partnership. Acceptance, on the other hand, promotes understanding, respect, and growth—for both you and the other person.

The Power of Acceptance

Acceptance does not imply passive resignation. It is not about giving up on someone or allowing unpleasant behavior to go unchecked. Instead, it is about acknowledging and honoring the natural autonomy of others. It entails recognizing individuals for who they are, with all their talents, weaknesses, oddities, and inconsistencies, and accepting that their life path may vary from what you imagine for them.

Acceptance may have a transforming effect. When you let people be themselves, you create a safe environment for authenticity. People are more likely to prosper when they feel accepted for who they are, rather than who they believe they should be to suit others. As a result, this sincerity improves your relationships. Genuine relationships are based on mutual respect, not force or manipulation.

Real-world examples of Acceptance

1. The Parent-Child Relationship

The parent-child relationship is one of the most powerful instances of the necessity of acceptance. Many parents struggle with allowing their children to make their own choices, especially if such decisions contradict the parent's ideals or wants. A parent may wish their kid to pursue a certain vocation, have certain religious views, or meet scholastic or social standards. However, enforcing these demands might cause friction and drive the youngster away, developing bitterness rather than intimacy.

Parents who learn to embrace their children for who they are, including their diverse ambitions, identities, and personalities, typically find that their connection strengthens. The youngster feels more comfortable revealing their actual self, and the parent enjoys experiencing their child's honest path. This is not to say that parents cannot lead or advise their children; but, effective guidance comes with the awareness that their responsibility is to support, not dictate, their child's path.

2) Romantic Relationships

It is common in love relationships to wish to "fix" or "improve" your companion. Perhaps you wish they were more ambitious, more organized, or shared your interests. These urges are normal, but when they cause stress or discontent, they may weaken the link. Constantly attempting to modify a spouse might make them feel inadequate, resulting in insecurity and emotional isolation.

However, accepting your partner's individuality helps both of you to feel appreciated for who you are. Accepting that your spouse may not always reflect your idealized picture of them allows you to appreciate the qualities and distinctions they offer to the partnership. It also decreases conflict since both partners feel safe in the knowledge that they are loved and appreciated for who they are, rather than who they could become following a series of changes.

3. Workplace dynamics

Learning to embrace coworkers' different working styles, personalities, and problem-solving techniques may lead to more productive cooperation in the workplace. Micromanaging or expecting everyone to follow your method of doing things may inhibit creativity and motivation. Teams that value individual abilities while respecting various work methods tend to be more inventive and efficient.

The Role of Boundaries

While welcoming people is necessary, it is also critical to set and maintain limits. Acceptance does not imply condoning damaging or disrespectful behavior. It is possible to respect someone's liberty while safeguarding your own emotional and mental health.

For example, you may accept that a buddy is unreliable and often cancels arrangements at the last minute. Instead of always being disappointed or attempting to alter them, you may modify your expectations. Perhaps you just arrange informal plans with this person, knowing their propensity to cancel, and save more organized gatherings for others who are more reliable. In this manner, you may safeguard your mental health without being resentful or upset by your friend's actions.

Boundaries also play an important role in more serious situations, such as partnerships involving emotional manipulation or poisonous behavior. Accepting someone as they are does not imply allowing oneself to be abused. In certain instances, acceptance may include acknowledging that the individual is unlikely to change and deciding to restrict or terminate the connection for your own well-being.

Strategies for Accepting Others' Uniqueness
1. Practice Empathy.

Understanding where someone is coming from is the first step towards acceptance. Consider: What experiences or ideas are influencing their behavior? How may their history influence their present actions? Empathy permits you to go beyond your viewpoint and comprehend the nuances of another person's existence.

2. Let go of control

Recognize that you can only manage how you respond to people. This does not imply being inactive; rather, it is acknowledging that people have the freedom to live their lives according to their own beliefs and choices, even if you disagree with them. Letting out of control lessens frustration and promotes happy relationships.

3. Adjust Your Expectations.

Frequently, disappointment originates from missed expectations. You may avoid the emotional toll of attempting to influence people by changing your expectations to be more realistic. Accept that others will make errors, have bad days, and behave in ways that upset you. Adjusting your expectations makes you more adaptable in relationships.

4. Focus on the Positive

Instead of dwelling on what you wish you could alter in someone, concentrate on what you like about them. What strengths do they provide to your relationship? What distinguishing characteristics brighten your life? Shifting your emphasis to a person's good qualities promotes appreciation and acceptance.

5. Practice Mindfulness

Mindfulness teaches us how to be present in the moment and notice our thoughts without judgment. When you have the desire to alter someone, halt and consider. Consider why you feel the need for change and if it is actually in the best interests of the other person—or whether it is motivated by your own discomfort with their behavior. Mindfulness permits you to react to events with more awareness and less impulsivity.

A Foundation for Acceptance
Learning to accept people for who they are is a lifelong exercise that may lead to deeper, more rewarding relationships. Acceptance does not imply forsaking one's own needs or tolerating destructive behavior. Instead, it is about letting go of the impulse to dominate people, accepting their differences, and keeping healthy boundaries that respect both your and their individuality.

Finally, when we allow individuals to be themselves, we relieve ourselves of the load of false expectations, making room for genuine connection, development, and mutual respect. Acceptance becomes not just an act of compassion towards others, but also a gift to ourselves— one that promotes inner peace and stronger, more fulfilling relationships.

Breaking Free from Approval-Seeking

Learning to live without the need for acceptance from others is one of the most freeing yet difficult life skills. We often find ourselves locked in a loop of seeking affirmation, whether from family, friends, coworkers, or even strangers on social media. This continuous search for acceptance may control our decisions, alter our behaviors, and eventually deprive us of our sense of ourselves. However, there is a way out. By adopting what is known as the Freedom Formula, you may begin to break free from the grasp of approval-seeking and cultivate an unshakeable feeling of internal validation and confidence.

Understanding the Freedom Formula.

The Freedom Formula is a simple yet deep concept: Let others think, feel, and do whatever they want—because it's none of your business. When you stop worrying about other people's thoughts and judgments, you recover your authority. Their approval—or lack thereof—does not define your value, nor do their judgments determine the course of your life. This notion advises us to let go of the desire to control how others see us and instead concentrate on living genuinely, by our beliefs and real selves.

The concept of allowing individuals to express their views and opinions without having to change or pacify them might seem radical. Many of us are conditioned from a young age to seek approval. We grow up in circumstances that encourage excellent behavior while criticizing deviations from cultural standards. Over time, our need for acceptance becomes ingrained, influencing how we behave, what we pursue, and even how we see ourselves.

The Trap of Approval Seeking

Seeking approval isn't necessarily negative. As social beings, we have a natural need to fit in, be liked, and belong. However, when the demand for acceptance is vital to our sense of self, it becomes a trap. The issue is its ephemeral nature— approval is often conditional, transient, and beyond our control. You might exhaust yourself trying to fulfill the expectations of others, only to discover that what was previously appreciated is now being criticized, or that the acceptance you get is false.

Approval-seeking may have negative repercussions. It stifles authenticity because we tend to shape ourselves to meet the preferences of others rather than seeking what is actually important to us. It causes anxiety because we continually worry about how others see us, which leads to overthinking and self-doubt. It also inhibits personal progress by making us scared to take chances or disrupt the status quo for fear of being rejected.

The Freedom of Letting Go.

The Freedom Formula asks us to let go of our desire for other people's acceptance. When you let others think, feel, and behave as they see fit—without making their views the center of your self-worth—you begin to feel a tremendous feeling of freedom. This independence stems from the realization that external approval is not required nor guaranteed for a fulfilling existence. Instead, you focus inside, developing your feeling of affirmation and self-worth.

Allowing people to be who they are gives you the freedom to be who you are. You are no longer burdened with attempting to meet someone else's standards.

This transformation enables you to live truly, make choices based on your beliefs, and pursue objectives that offer you real fulfillment. This allows you to move away from a life of perpetual compromise and towards one that is your own.

Building Internal Validation

Breaking away from approval-seeking requires developing inner validation. This process entails establishing a strong sense of self-worth that is not dependent on external praise or acknowledgment. Here are some major ways to develop internal validation:

1 Know Your Values

Inner validation is built on a clear understanding of your beliefs. When you understand what is important to you—whether it's honesty, creativity, compassion, or independence—you can make choices that are consistent with these values, regardless of what others think. Defining your basic beliefs helps you remain grounded and focused on creating a meaningful life for yourself, rather than one formed by the changeable views of others.

2. Practice Self-Compassion.

Learning to be gentle with oneself is an important aspect of letting go of the need for approval. Self-compassion is treating oneself with the same understanding and care you would provide to a good friend. Instead of severely condemning oneself for errors or apparent failures, you show yourself kindness and support. This practice increases resilience and reduces your need for external validation since you know you are deserving of love and acceptance from yourself regardless of your circumstances.

3. Create Boundaries with Others

A lack of boundaries often leads to approval-seeking behavior. We may say yes when we wish to say no or adjust our minds to fit others around us. Setting boundaries entails being honest about your limitations and not sacrificing your principles or well-being for acceptance. It also entails understanding that other people's expectations or views are not your responsibility. Setting hard limits protects your authenticity and gives you the freedom to live by your standards.

4. Celebrate Your Own Achievements

Becoming your own greatest cheerleader is an effective method to overcome the urge for approval. Instead of waiting for people to recognize your successes, take the time to celebrate your personal development, no matter how modest. Recognize your efforts whether you've done a challenging assignment at work, met a personal goal, or just gotten through a difficult day. Self-celebration promotes the message that you are enough as you are, without the need for external approval.

5. Stop People-Pleasing.

People-pleasing is the direct effect of approval-seeking. To avoid confrontation or rejection, we engage in people-pleasing behaviors such as agreeing to do things we do not want to do, repressing our ideas, or going out of our way to make others comfortable. However, this comes at the expense of our pleasure and authenticity. Breaking away from people-pleasing entails learning to say no, communicate your demands, and advocate for your own goals, even if it means disappointing others.

Real-Life Examples of Breaking Free From Approval Seeking

1. Career Change

Sarah had always intended to pursue a creative career in art, but she worked in a corporate environment for years to support her family's financial needs. Despite her external accomplishments, she felt dissatisfied and alienated from herself. After years of chasing her parents' approval, Sarah resolved to let go of their expectations and pursue her passion. While her family originally objected, Sarah's choice to prioritize her pleasure led to a successful career as an artist. By accepting the Freedom Formula, she realized that her family's views did not determine her value or success.

2. Social media detox

John was always checking social media to see how many likes and comments his postings had garnered. He found himself shaping his material to what he believed people would like, rather than expressing what was important to him. Over time, this behavior caused emotions of inadequacy and worry. John decided to take a vacation from social media and work on his pursuits without seeking external reinforcement. This detox helped him reconnect with his inner hobbies and see that his value was not dependent on the amount of likes he got. He learned to allow others to express their thoughts while focusing on his feeling of fulfillment.

3. A Romantic Relationship

Emily had always felt compelled to meet her partner's standards, fearful that if she did not, he would leave her. She modified her activities, avoided certain subjects of discussion, and even changed her look to suit his tastes. But the more she wanted his approval, the more she felt estranged from her own identity. Emily eventually realized that she couldn't keep sacrificing her own happiness for the sake of the relationship. She accepted the Freedom Formula, believing that if her spouse couldn't accept her for who she was, they weren't in the appropriate relationship. Letting go of her need for acceptance enabled her to establish a relationship in which she could be herself.

The Impact of Self-Confidence

The development of self-confidence is important to break away from the need for acceptance. True confidence comes from understanding and believing oneself, regardless of what others think. It is the capacity to be confident in your views, values, and judgments without relying on external confirmation to feel comfortable. When you have self-confidence, you recognize that your value is intrinsic—it cannot be given or taken away based on someone else's view.

Building self-confidence needs constant practice. It entails confronting your anxieties of rejection or disapproval and discovering that you can live, even flourish, without the acceptance of others. When you make a choice based on your ideals rather than others' expectations, you boost your self-esteem and independence.

The Power of Inner Validation

Breaking away from approval-seeking is one of the most liberating journeys you can take. By accepting the Freedom Formula and focusing on inner affirmation, you may break free from the grueling cycle of striving to fulfill others' expectations. This approach needs fortitude, self-awareness, and a willingness to accept pain, but the benefits are enormous. You'll feel a renewed feeling of freedom, confidence, and authenticity, allowing you to live a life true to yourself.

Finally, when you stop seeking approval from others, you open the door to deeper, more meaningful relationships—ones built on mutual respect rather than the desire for affirmation. You learn to trust yourself, enjoy your achievements, and make choices that are consistent with your beliefs. By doing so, you not only liberate yourself from the constraints of external judgment, but you also develop a life full of purpose, passion, and self-acceptance.

Letting Go in Relationships

Relationships are the foundation of our life, offering love, support, and companionship. However, they may also cause irritation, conflict, and disappointment when we attempt to control or modify people to meet our expectations. Romantic relationships, friendships, and family dynamics all provide chances for connection and development, but each needs a careful balance of limits, acceptance, and trust. The Freedom Formula offers a strong paradigm for negotiating these interactions in ways that promote authenticity, minimize conflict, and enhance emotional attachments.

By using the Freedom Formula in your relationships, you eliminate the desire for control and allow individuals to be themselves, without the continual impulse to correct, transform, or mold them into an idealized version that meets your needs. This allows for better, more true interactions built on mutual respect and acceptance rather than artificial expectations.

The Challenge of Control in Relationships

Control often emerges in relationships when we have a preconceived notion of how others should act, think, or feel. We may expect our spouse to behave in a specific manner, our friends to share our values, or our family members to satisfy certain criteria. When these expectations are not realized, it may result in disappointment, anger, and conflict. This desire for control may manifest in subtle ways, such as providing unsolicited advice, continually criticizing, or attempting to "fix" people when we believe they are failing to fulfill our expectations.

However, control in relationships is inevitably restrictive. It denies individuals the freedom to be themselves and stifles the possibility of meaningful connection. Instead of embracing individuals for who they are, we concentrate on how they might or should be. Over time, this dynamic may erode trust, create distance, and eventually undermine the relationship. When we let go of control and embrace the Freedom Formula, we create more freedom, trust, and understanding.

Letting Go of Romantic Partnerships

Control concerns are often seen in romantic relationships. We place a high value on our spouses and often expect them to supply all of our emotional, psychological, and spiritual demands. However, these high expectations may put unnecessary strain on a relationship and lead to dissatisfaction when they are not realized.

Applying the Freedom Formula in a love relationship entails acknowledging that your partner is a unique person with their wants, interests, and ways of existing in the world. Instead of attempting to modify people to fit your idealized picture, you accept them as they are, warts and all. This should not imply condoning bad behavior or surrendering your ideals. Instead, it is letting go of the need to regulate how individuals express themselves, live their lives, or deal with their emotions.

For example:

- Acceptance of Differences: If you and your spouse have different methods of dealing with stress or communication, rather than attempting to "correct" them to fit your style, you may learn to embrace and respect these differences. For the connection to flourish, their approach does not need to be the same as yours.

- Avoiding the Fixer Role: Many individuals get into the trap of attempting to "fix" their partner's perceived flaws, such as emotional availability, professional choices, or social behaviors. The Freedom Formula urges you to walk away from the fixer position and let your spouse have the dignity of making their own decisions and navigating their own development path.

In love relationships, letting up control allows for mutual respect and personal development. Your spouse feels noticed and cherished for who they are, rather than what they may become under your influence. This establishes a foundation of trust and emotional safety, which are required for long-term and meaningful relationships.

Letting Go of Friendships

Friendships flourish on shared experiences, ideals, and emotional support, but they may also be strained by differences in lifestyle, priorities, or viewpoints. In our need to feel close to our friends, we may attempt to influence their decisions or expect them to act in ways that are consistent with our own. When such expectations are not satisfied, this may lead to irritation and, in some cases, the friendship breaking apart.

Applying the Freedom Formula to friendships entails allowing your friends to live their lives as they see fit. It entails accepting that your pals will not always make the same choices you do, and that's alright. You may maintain a close relationship without forcing your ideals, ideas, or expectations on others.

Consider the following scenarios:

- Different Life Choices: Perhaps a buddy makes a decision that you disagree with, such as relocating to a new place, pursuing a hazardous job shift, or joining a relationship that you believe is not good for them. Rather than attempting to persuade someone to reconsider their choice, the Let someone Theory instructs you to respect their autonomy. Even if their decisions seem hazardous or wrong to you, it is critical to accept their freedom to choose their path.

- Accepting Differences in Priorities: As friendships develop, priorities may vary. Perhaps your buddy is now more focused on their family or work, which leaves less time for socializing. Rather than feeling slighted or attempting to shame them into spending more time with you, the Freedom Formula advises you to accept their shifting priorities without taking it personally. This acceptance may lead to a stronger, more understanding relationship, even if the friendship appears different than it did before.

Letting go of friendships does not imply that you stop caring or lower your standards. Instead, it's about appreciating your friend's originality and encouraging their personal development, even if it differs from your expectations.

Letting Go in Family Dynamics.

Family ties may be among the most complex and emotionally intense interactions we have. Family dynamics, whether imposed by parents, siblings, or extended relatives, may produce a feeling of responsibility, pressure, or even animosity when others fail to fulfill the roles we've given them. This is particularly true when we feel compelled to regulate or influence family members' decisions, whether they are about a parent's health, a sibling's work, or a relative's parenting style.

The Freedom Formula may be an effective technique for improving family relationships by removing the urge to manage or influence your family members. Here's how to use it in typical household scenarios:

- Parental Expectations: Many individuals struggle to match their parents' expectations for them, whether it's about their work, lifestyle, or family. By using the Freedom Formula, you may start to divorce your identity from your parents' approval. This does not imply cutting relationships or rejecting your family's ideals, but rather letting go of the urge to meet their vision for your life. You are free to follow your path, even if it deviates from what they envisioned.

- Siblings and Rivalry: Sibling relationships can include deep-seated comparisons, rivalries, or expectations of loyalty. In this context, letting go implies allowing your siblings to live their own lives, make their own mistakes, and follow their aspirations without comparing them to you or expecting them to match specific criteria. This allows for more genuine interactions, in which sibling attachments are built on mutual support rather than rivalry or disappointed expectations.

- Relinquishing Influence Over Adult Children: As their children mature into adults, parents often struggle to let go of the urge to guide, counsel, or influence their choices. The Freedom Formula may be very helpful here. Accepting that your adult children are capable of making their own decisions—even if they vary from what you would recommend—allows them to develop their own identities. Instead of frequent interference or criticism, this may help to build the parent-child connection by establishing respect and mutual trust.

 Reducing Conflict by Letting Go

Unmet expectations or a desire to control how others act are common sources of conflict in partnerships. When we anticipate our partners, friends, or family members to behave in a certain manner and they do not, we feel upset, disappointed, or even betrayed. Here's where letting go might be beneficial. By accepting the Freedom Formula, you decrease the friction that comes from attempting to force your will on others.

Letting go does not imply avoiding confrontation at all costs or ignoring your wants. Instead, it is determining which conflicts are worth waging and knowing when to relinquish control. It's about realizing that everyone has their path and trusting them to manage it without your continual supervision.

For example:

- Reducing Arguments in Romantic Relationships: When you quit attempting to influence or control your partner's behavior, you avoid many unneeded conflicts. Instead of attempting to "win" an argument, you might work on understanding your partner's point of view and establishing common ground. Letting go fosters an environment of collaboration and mutual respect, lowering the severity and frequency of confrontations.

- Avoiding Power Conflicts in Friendships: Friendships may sometimes descend into power conflicts about who is right, who is more successful, or whose viewpoint is more important. The Freedom Formula pushes you to let go of your need to compete or control. By accepting your friends' diversity and honoring their journeys, you may foster a more peaceful and helpful connection.

- De-escalating Tension at Family reunions: Family reunions may be fraught with old emotions and unsolved disputes. Applying the Freedom Formula in these instances entails letting go of the desire to prove a point or win an argument. Instead, you concentrate on maintaining a calm and courteous environment, even if there are ongoing arguments or differences of opinion.

Developing Healthier, More Authentic Relationships

When you use the Freedom Formula in your relationships, you foster better, more real interactions built on mutual respect and understanding. By surrendering the urge for control, you create room for authentic engagement without the burden of meeting artificial expectations.

In romantic relationships, this leads to increased emotional closeness since both parties feel accepted for who they are rather than who they are supposed to be. Friendships foster a loving and mutually fulfilling relationship in which both parties feel free to develop and progress without fear of judgment or pressure. In family relations, letting go leads to more polite and peaceful interactions as you learn to accept your loved one's decisions, even if they vary from your own.

One of the most powerful benefits of the Freedom Formula is the ability to develop honest relationships. When you stop attempting to alter others, you allow them to be themselves—flawed, unique, and human. This does not imply that you condone harmful behavior or tolerate conditions that jeopardize your well-being, but rather that you establish limits while respecting others' individuality.

Effective Strategies for Letting Go in Relationships

While the concept of letting go may seem straightforward, it may be difficult to put into action, particularly in deeply rooted relationships. Here are some practical techniques for implementing the Freedom Formula in your relationships:

1. Set Clear Boundaries: Letting go does not imply

allowing someone to cross your boundaries or compromise your principles. In reality, having clear boundaries is critical for preserving your mental well-being while enabling others to make their own decisions. Define what behaviors are unacceptable to you, then convey them gently and explicitly.

2. Practice Active Listening: Rather than attempting to force your ideas or thoughts, concentrate on actually listening to others. Active listening enables you to understand where they are coming from and react with empathy rather than judgment. This increases trust and deepens your relationship.

3. Release Expectations: Try to recognize your expectations of others, whether they should act, believe, or respond to you. Recognize that these expectations are based on your viewpoint and may not

reflect their reality. By letting go of these expectations, you take pressure off the relationship.

4. Focus on Your Growth: Instead of attempting to influence others, concentrate on your personal growth. Consider how you can become more welcoming, kind, and understanding. The more you focus on your development, the less you will feel the urge to dominate others.

5. Embrace Imperfection: Everyone, including you, is flawed. Accept that individuals make errors, and those faults do not define them or the relationship. Embracing imperfection allows for greater connection and understanding.

6. Leave the Need to Be Correct: In many disagreements, the need to be correct exacerbates tension and animosity. Practice letting go of the need to "win" disputes or establish a point. Instead, prioritize the

health of the connection above correctness.

7. Allow for Change and Evolution: People develop and evolve throughout time. Rather than rejecting these changes or clinging to an obsolete version of someone, accept their progress. This flexibility enriches your partnership by allowing room for development and adaptability.

Letting go in relationships does not imply detachment or apathy; rather, it entails establishing the circumstances for genuine, meaningful interactions founded on respect and acceptance. The Freedom Formula tells us that abandoning our desire for control fosters greater trust, reduces conflict, and leads to stronger, more harmonious relationships with the people in our lives.

Whether in love, friendship, or familial relationship, letting go allows for deeper emotional closeness, less friction, and a firmer basis for long-term connection. Allowing individuals to be themselves—without continual interference or correction—creates room for love, understanding, and mutual progress.

Letting go does not imply disengaging or avoiding unpleasant talks; rather, it entails embracing individuals for who they are and acknowledging that your purpose is not to alter them, but to help them on their path. When you use this technique in your relationships, you release yourself from the tiresome urge to control and instead enjoy the beauty of relationships that thrive in an atmosphere of acceptance and mutual respect.

Transforming Failure and Rejection

Failure and rejection are common experiences, but they have an emotional weight that often causes emotions of guilt, despair, and aggravation. When we don't get the results we want or when people reject us— whether in our personal or professional lives—it's simple to internalize these events as a reflection of our value. However, embracing the Freedom Formula may fundamentally alter how we see and react to failure and rejection, changing these setbacks into chances for development and self-discovery.

The Freedom Formula revolves around the idea of letting go—not just of the urge to control others, but also of the need to control results. Failure and rejection are typically unpleasant because we are connected to particular outcomes. We want achievement, validation, approval, or acceptance, and when we do not get these, it seems like a personal assault. But what if failure and rejection were not signs of insufficiency, but rather turning points that guided us along a better road for our growth?

Redefining Failure and Rejection.

Traditionally, failure and rejection were considered undesirable consequences that should be avoided at all costs. However, letting go of our anxiety about these events allows us to get a larger perspective. Failure does not represent our value or ability; it is just feedback. Rejection is not an indication that we are not good enough; it is a redirection.

The first step in healing your connection with failure and rejection is to rethink what these events mean to you. Rather than perceiving them as dead ends, consider their chances for progress. Every time you fail, you learn something new about yourself, your strategy, or the scenario. Each rejection provides insight, directing you away from routes that aren't suited for you and towards those that are.

The Role of Letting Go

Letting go does not imply giving up on your objectives or admitting failure; rather, it entails abandoning your connection to a certain result. We sometimes devote so much emotional energy to reaching a certain outcome that when things do not go as planned, it seems heartbreaking. The Freedom Formula instructs us to let go of our need for things to happen in a specific manner. This separation from the result permits us to stay open to the new possibilities and lessons that failure and rejection might provide.

When you let go of your desire for achievement or acceptability, you relieve yourself of the worry and pressure that comes with those expectations. Instead of dreading failure, you approach it with interest. Instead of anticipating rejection, you see it as a chance to pursue another route.

Moving from External Validation to Internal Growth

Failure and rejection are particularly painful because we often seek approval from outside sources. We want acceptance from others to feel worthwhile, and we judge our success based on external accomplishments. However, our dependence on external validation exposes us to feelings of disappointment when we do not achieve the desired goals.

The Freedom Formula emphasizes the significance of transitioning from external validation to internal progress. When you let go of the desire for others' approval or for things to come out a particular way, you cease basing your value on external events. Instead, you start measuring your progress based on how much you've learned, how resilient you've become, and how eager you are to take on new difficulties.

Failure and rejection become less painful when you concentrate on your improvement. You start to perceive them as milestones in the path rather than defining events. The question has changed from "Did I succeed?" or "Was I accepted?" to "What did I learn?" and "How can I grow from this?"

Viewing Failure as a Catalyst of Growth

One of the most dramatic changes that may occur when you accept the Freedom Formula is learning to see failure as a stimulus for progress. Some of history's greatest triumphs sprang from repeated failures. Consider visionaries like Thomas Edison, who famously failed hundreds of times before creating the lightbulb, or sportsmen who endured several failures before reaching their peak.

What distinguishes successful individuals from others who stay trapped in their failures is not the lack of setbacks, but their will to persevere and learn from them. Letting go of your fear of failure helps you to take chances, knowing that even if things don't go as planned, you'll be wiser and more equipped for the next challenge.

The Gift of Rejection.

Rejection, although painful, may be a blessing. It challenges us to rethink our objectives, assess our aspirations, and refocus our efforts on routes that better reflect who we are. In relationships, rejection might help us figure out what kinds of connections we need. In our professions, rejection might lead us to previously unconsidered prospects.

When you embrace the Freedom Formula and let go of the desire for other people's acceptance, rejection becomes less personal. You understand that someone's choice to reject you isn't always a reflection of your value, but rather a hint that you and the other person, job, or scenario were not a good match. In this sense, rejection is a redirection towards something more conducive to your progress and fulfillment.

Detaching from Outcomes: A Way to Freedom

Detaching from precise results is one of the Freedom Formula's most freeing characteristics. When you let go of the urge for things to come out a specific way, you may avoid disappointment and irritation. This does not imply that you should stop caring or trying for achievement; rather, you should approach your objectives with an open mind and a readiness to accept whatever happens.

This detachment also helps you to take larger chances because you know that failure is not the end of the story—it's just part of the journey. By letting go of the impulse to control outcomes, you gain emotional freedom and resilience. You become more adaptive, ready to change course when things don't go as planned, and more open to new chances.

Practical Steps to Let Go of Failure and Rejection

To completely modify how you handle failure and rejection, you may take the following practical steps:

1. Reframe Setbacks as Learning Opportunities: When you face failure or rejection, ask yourself what you can learn from the experience. Write down the lessons and consider how they will help you develop or grow.

2. Practice self-compassion: Be kind to yourself when things don't go as planned. Recognize that everyone has setbacks, and they do not determine your value or ability. Self-compassion allows you to go on with more resilience.

3. Release the Need for Control: Remind yourself that you cannot control everything, particularly the actions or choices of others.

Concentrate on what you can control: your attitude, effort, and reaction to adversity.

4. Promote Inner Validation: Change your attention from seeking external acceptance to developing your self-esteem from the inside. Celebrate your success, no matter how tiny, and recognize the work you put into your endeavors, regardless of the results.

5. Adopt a progress Mindset: Be open to the idea that failure and rejection are necessary for progress. Instead of perceiving them as failures, consider them stepping stones on your path to achievement.

Failure and rejection are unavoidable, but how you react may make all the difference. By accepting the Freedom Formula and letting go of your connection to certain outcomes, you may turn these experiences into great chances for personal growth and development.

When you overcome your fear of failure, you unlock your ability to take chances, try new things, and pursue your objectives with bravery and perseverance. When you cease depending on external validation, rejection loses its ability to undermine your feeling of value. Instead, you view it as a guide, directing you to the people, opportunities, and experiences that are intended for you.

Finally, failure and rejection are not obstacles to achievement; they are necessary components of the path. By letting go, you liberate yourself from the emotional burden of these events and open yourself up to the boundless possibilities that await. Failure and rejection are common experiences, but they have an emotional weight that often causes emotions of guilt, despair, and aggravation. When we don't get the results we want or when people reject us—whether in our personal or professional lives—it's simple to internalize these events as a reflection of our value. However, embracing the Freedom Formula may fundamentally alter how we see and react to failure and rejection, changing these setbacks into chances for development and self-discovery.

The Freedom Formula revolves around the idea of letting go—not just of the urge to control others, but also of the need to control results. Failure and rejection are typically unpleasant because we are connected to particular outcomes. We want achievement, validation, approval, or acceptance, and when we do not get these, it seems like a personal assault. But what if failure and rejection were not signs of insufficiency, but rather turning points that guided us along a better road for our growth?

Redefining Failure and Rejection.

Traditionally, failure and rejection were considered undesirable consequences that should be avoided at all costs. However, letting go of our anxiety about these events allows us to get a larger perspective. Failure does not represent our value or ability; it is just feedback. Rejection is not an indication that we are not good enough; it is a redirection.

The first step in healing your connection with failure and rejection is to rethink what these events mean to you. Rather than perceiving them as dead ends, consider their chances for progress. Every time you fail, you learn something new about yourself, your strategy, or the scenario. Each rejection provides insight, directing you away from routes that aren't suited for you and towards those that are.

The Role of Letting Go

Letting go does not imply giving up on your objectives or admitting failure; rather, it entails abandoning your connection to a certain result. We sometimes devote so much emotional energy to reaching a certain outcome that when things do not go as planned, it seems heartbreaking. The Freedom Formula instructs us to let go of our need for things to happen in a specific manner. This separation from the result permits us to stay open to the new possibilities and lessons that failure and rejection might provide.

When you let go of your desire for achievement or acceptability, you relieve yourself of the worry and pressure that comes with those expectations. Instead of dreading failure, you approach it with interest. Instead of anticipating rejection, you see it as a chance to pursue another route.

Moving from External Validation to Internal Growth

Failure and rejection are particularly painful because we often seek approval from outside sources. We want acceptance from others to feel worthwhile, and we judge our success based on external accomplishments. However, our dependence on external validation exposes us to feelings of disappointment when we do not achieve the desired goals.

The Freedom Formula emphasizes the significance of transitioning from external validation to internal progress. When you let go of the desire for others' approval or for things to come out a particular way, you cease basing your value on external events. Instead, you start measuring your progress based on how much you've learned, how resilient you've become, and how eager you are to take on new difficulties.

Failure and rejection become less painful when you

concentrate on your improvement. You start to perceive them as milestones in the path rather than defining events. The question has changed from "Did I succeed?" or "Was I accepted?" to "What did I learn?" and "How can I grow from this?"

Viewing Failure as a Catalyst of Growth

One of the most dramatic changes that may occur when you accept the Freedom Formula is learning to see failure as a stimulus for progress. Some of history's greatest triumphs sprang from repeated failures. Consider visionaries like Thomas Edison, who famously failed hundreds of times before creating the lightbulb, or sportsmen who endured several failures before reaching their peak.

What distinguishes successful individuals from others who stay trapped in their failures is not the lack of setbacks, but their will to persevere and learn from them. Letting go of your fear of failure helps you to take chances, knowing that even if things don't go as planned, you'll be wiser and more equipped for the next challenge.

The Gift of Rejection.

Rejection, although painful, may be a blessing. It challenges us to rethink our objectives, assess our aspirations, and refocus our efforts on routes that better reflect who we are. In relationships, rejection might help us figure out what kinds of connections we need. In our professions, rejection might lead us to previously unconsidered prospects.

When you embrace the Freedom Formula and let go of the desire for other people's acceptance, rejection becomes less personal. You understand that someone's choice to reject you isn't always a reflection of your value, but rather a hint that you and the other person, job, or scenario were not a good match. In this sense, rejection is a redirection towards something more conducive to your progress and fulfillment.

Detaching from Outcomes: A Way to Freedom

Detaching from precise results is one of the Freedom Formula's most freeing characteristics. When you let go of the urge for things to come out a specific way, you may avoid disappointment and irritation. This does not imply that you should stop caring or trying for achievement; rather, you should approach your objectives with an open mind and a readiness to accept whatever happens.

This detachment also helps you to take larger chances because you know that failure is not the end of the story—it's just part of the journey. By letting go of the impulse to control outcomes, you gain emotional freedom and resilience. You become more adaptive, ready to change course when things don't go as planned, and more open to new chances.

Practical Steps to Let Go of Failure and Rejection

To completely modify how you handle failure and rejection, you may take the following practical steps:

1. Reframe Setbacks as Learning Opportunities: When you face failure or rejection, ask yourself what you can learn from the experience. Write down the lessons and consider how they will help you develop or grow.

2. Practice self-compassion: Be kind to yourself when things don't go as planned. Recognize that everyone has setbacks, and they do not determine your value or ability. Self-compassion allows you to go on with more resilience.

3. Release the Need for Control: Remind yourself that you cannot control everything, particularly the actions or choices of others. Concentrate on what you can

control: your attitude, effort, and reaction to adversity.

4. Promote Inner Validation: Change your attention from seeking external acceptance to developing your self-esteem from the inside. Celebrate your success, no matter how tiny, and recognize the work you put into your endeavors, regardless of the results.

5. Adopt a progress Mindset: Be open to the idea that failure and rejection are necessary for progress. Instead of perceiving them as failures, consider them stepping stones on your path to achievement.

Failure and rejection are unavoidable, but how you react may make all the difference. By accepting the Freedom Formula and letting go of your connection to certain outcomes, you may turn these experiences into great chances for personal growth and development.

When you overcome your fear of failure, you unlock your

ability to take chances, try new things, and pursue your objectives with bravery and perseverance. When you cease depending on external validation, rejection loses its ability to undermine your feeling of value. Instead, you view it as a guide, directing you to the people, opportunities, and experiences that are intended for you.

Finally, failure and rejection are not obstacles to achievement; they are necessary components of the path. By letting go, you liberate yourself from the emotional burden of these events and open yourself up to the boundless possibilities that await.

Living in Alignment with the Freedom Formula

The Freedom Formula promotes a radical change in

thinking, encouraging us to let go of the impulse to control people, results, and even our responses to life's obstacles. It encourages independence, acceptance, and the capacity to live in harmony with oneself and others around us. But how do you get from comprehending the theory to truly using it in your daily life?

In this last chapter, we'll look at real, tangible strategies to help you incorporate the Freedom Formula into your everyday choices, relationships, and long-term objectives. These methods will improve your mental and emotional well-being while also leading to a more satisfying, balanced, and honest existence.

1. Begin with self-awareness

The first and most critical step in aligning with the Freedom Formula is to become self-aware. You must recognize when you are too controlling, whether in relationships, at business, or with personal ambitions.

- Daily Reflections: Take a few minutes at the end of each day to think about times when you may have attempted to control people or results. Consider the following questions: "Did I impose my expectations on someone today?" or, "Was I attached to a specific result that caused me stress?" Journaling your thoughts might help you become more aware of these times.

- Watch Your Reactions: Throughout the day, observe your internal responses to circumstances. Do you experience anxiety or frustration when things do not go as planned? Do you feel compelled to interfere when others do not reach your expectations? This knowledge will provide the groundwork for transformation.

2. Practice Detachment from Results

Living in accordance with the Freedom Formula entails letting go of the desire for certain results, particularly those that are beyond your control. Detaching from outcomes helps you to appreciate the process of living and working without the continual pressure to achieve specific results.

- Focus on the process, not the outcome: Whether you're working on a project or chasing a goal, shift your emphasis away from the final product and onto the journey. Enjoy the effort, the learning, and the progress that it brings. This reduces the emotional cost of probable failure or disappointment.

- Release the "What Ifs": Our connection to results is often motivated by a dread of what may go wrong. Practice releasing these "what if" situations by reminding yourself that you cannot anticipate or control everything. When you let go of these imaginary fears, you make room for greater serenity and creativity in your life.

3. Create Healthy Boundaries
One common misperception about the Freedom Formula is that it promotes passivity or allows others to walk all over you. On the contrary, living by this notion necessitates establishing healthy limits. Accepting people as they are does not imply enabling them to push your boundaries or sacrifice your principles.

- Identify Your Limits: Consider what behaviors or circumstances you're prepared to tolerate and what you're not. Clear limits are necessary for both personal and professional interactions. For example, if a buddy is constantly late or unreliable, you may choose to accept this as part of their personality while still establishing limits around how much time you spend waiting for them or relying on them.

- Communicate Clearly. Once you've determined your limits, explain them calmly and respectfully. For example, in the workplace, if you feel swamped with duties, communicate your boundaries and negotiate a more reasonable assignment. Boundaries are intended to preserve your well-being while enabling others to be themselves.

4. Embrace flexibility and adaptability

Living by the Freedom Formula entails accepting life's unpredictability and being flexible in your reactions. The more rigid your expectations, the more difficult it is to let go and adjust when things do not go as planned.

- Practice Adaptability When confronted with unanticipated developments, strive to see them as possibilities rather than setbacks. If your strategy fails, ask yourself, "What can I learn from this?" or "How can I pivot and move forward?" This thinking allows you to retain a feeling of control over your emotions even when external situations are out of your hands.

- Embrace Uncertainty: Life is full of uncertainty, and attempting to control everything is stressful and ineffective. Instead of opposing the unknown, try embracing it. Remind yourself that uncertainty may result in new possibilities, personal development, and unexpected advantages. The more you accept ambiguity, the less dread and worry you will experience.

5. Promote Acceptance in Relationships

One of the most effective uses of the Freedom Formula is in relationships. Accepting individuals for who they are, warts and all, may significantly enhance your relationships and lessen conflict.

- Give Up the Need to Change Others: Consider if you're attempting to shape the people in your life to conform to your expectations. Are you continually giving advice or providing unsolicited solutions? Instead, practice acceptance by letting people make their own decisions, even if they don't match your vision. This encourages respect and deeper connections.

- Focus on What You Control: In relationships, concentrate on your actions and emotions rather than attempting to influence the behavior of others. You cannot alter how others react, but you can control how you communicate, create boundaries, and manage your emotions. This allows you to preserve peace without the need to correct or change others.

6. Make Decisions With Clarity and Confidence

Living according to the Freedom Formula entails making choices based on confidence and clarity, rather than being swayed by the views of others or cultural expectations. Letting go entails eliminating the need for external validation in your decision-making processes.

- Trust Yourself: Begin to trust your judgment and instincts. When making choices, large or small, consider what you want, rather than what others expect of you. This allows you to honor your aspirations while also living more truthfully.

- Avoid overthinking: We may hesitate to make choices out of fear of failure or rejection. Practice making judgments swiftly and confidently, acknowledging that not every option will be ideal. The more you let go of overthinking, the more determined and powerful you will become.

7: Align Your Long-Term Goals With Inner Peace

Setting long-term objectives that promote inner serenity and fulfillment, rather than pursuing outward achievement or acceptance, is an important aspect of living by the Freedom Formula.

- Set Value-Based Goals: Instead of creating objectives

based purely on external successes, such as money or prestige, prioritize goals that are consistent with your basic beliefs. Consider the following questions: "What kind of life do I want to live?" Additionally, "What makes me feel fulfilled?" Setting objectives based on your principles leads to a more honest and meaningful existence.

- Detach from External Validation: When pursuing your objectives, remember that success is not defined by others' acknowledgment or appreciation. Whether or whether others approve of your route, stick to what seems right for you. This helps you escape the trap of seeking external affirmation and keeps you focused on your unique vision of success.

8. Be Patient and Compassionate

Living by the Freedom Formula requires patience— both with yourself and others. Personal improvement is a lifetime endeavor that must be approached with care and compassion.

- Be patient with yourself: Change does not happen quickly, and it is common to go back into old patterns of control or attachment. When this occurs, engage in self-compassion. Recognize that you are doing your best and that improvement is an ongoing process.

- Be Compassionate for Others: The same goes for the individuals around you. Others are on their paths of self-discovery and progress, just as you are learning to let go. Give them the same tolerance and understanding you give yourself.

Every day, we live by the Freedom Formula.

Incorporating the Freedom Formula into your life is a continuous process that involves attention, patience, and purpose. Building self-awareness, practicing detachment, creating boundaries, accepting flexibility, and aligning your objectives with your inner values are all doable activities that may help you live a more peaceful, genuine, and satisfying life.

As you go down this road, you will notice that your need to control people and results fades, replaced with a feeling of freedom and acceptance. Your relationships will be more harmonious, your objectives more meaningful, and your everyday life more enjoyable. Living by the Freedom Formula helps you to release unneeded control burdens and enjoy the beauty of spontaneous unfolding.

The process of completely adopting this attitude takes time, but each step leads you closer to a life of real serenity, freedom, and personal power. Allowing people to be who they are, as well as letting go of the consequences over which you have no control, allows you to live, freely, and in alignment with your truest self.

Conclusion

Throughout our lives, we are taught to seek control over our situations, relationships, occupations, and even our emotions. We are conditioned to think that by tightly controlling and methodically regulating every element of our life, we may obtain pleasure, prosperity, and safety. However, this obsessive desire for control often produces the opposite result: worry, tension, frustration, and dissatisfaction. In contrast, the Freedom Formula is simple yet profound: by letting go, we gain genuine pleasure, freedom, and fulfillment.

In this last section, we will look at how letting go may affect numerous elements of your life, bringing you closer to true peace and pleasure. We will also share our concluding views on how to use this transforming concept in your daily life.

Letting Go: The Key to Inner Peace.

At its foundation, the act of letting go is about giving up the illusion of control. It entails admitting that not everything in life is beyond our control—other people's actions, the results of our efforts, and even the unforeseen twists of life itself. When we let go of the need to manage every detail, we make room for serenity.

- Relief From Stress and Anxiety: One of the most visible advantages of letting go is a decrease in tension and anxiety. When you no longer feel the need to control every result or predict every potential issue, you may approach life with a feeling of peace. You learn to believe that things will develop as they should, without the need to push or force them.

- Live in the Present Moment: Letting go naturally takes you to the present moment. When you are no longer concerned with controlling the future or rewriting the past, you can completely participate in the present. This presence helps you to enjoy life's basic joys, such as the flavor of your morning coffee or the warmth of a meaningful discussion.

Embracing Uncertainty: A Path to Freedom

The Freedom Formula requires accepting life's inherent uncertainties. While it is human nature to want consistency and security, genuine freedom comes from surrendering the desire for promises. When you let go of your need for certainty, you open yourself up to the limitless possibilities that life has to offer.

- Opportunity for Development and Exploration: By letting go of inflexible expectations, you create space for personal development and discovery. Life becomes less about meeting predefined goals and more about finding new chances, learning from unforeseen difficulties, and growing as a person. This willingness to accept life's volatility stimulates your creativity and flexibility.

- Freedom From Fear: Fear typically stems from the unknown—what will happen if things don't go as planned? What happens if I fail? What happens if I am rejected? Letting go releases you from the hold of dread because you no longer expect things to go flawlessly. You gain confidence in your capacity to manage whatever comes your way, knowing that your value and happiness are not dependent on certain results.

Letting Go in Relationships: Building Healthier Connections

The power of letting go is most transformational in relationships. Attempting to control or modify people in love relationships, friendships, or family dynamics causes tension, frustration, and emotional tiredness. The Freedom Formula urges you to let go of this desire and embrace acceptance instead.

- Acceptance versus Control: When you let individuals be themselves rather than attempting to mold them into your expectations, you build deeper, more real connections. Acceptance creates trust and respect, which are essential components of lasting relationships. Letting up control helps people to be recognized and appreciated for who they genuinely are, rather than how they fit into your plans.

- Healthy boundaries: Letting go does not imply allowing someone to cross over your boundaries. It entails creating clear, healthy boundaries that safeguard your emotional and mental health while also respecting the autonomy of others. This balance makes relationships more enjoyable and less tiring.

Giving Up Control Over Results: Finding Joy in the Process

The constant pursuit of objectives might seem like a

marathon, with the finish line creeping further away. The Freedom Formula urges you to concentrate on the journey rather than the goal. By letting go of the demand for certain results, you may enjoy the process of living, working, and creating.

- Power of Presence: When you are no longer focused on reaching certain goals, you become more involved in the present. This presence increases fulfillment, whether you're working on a personal project, spending time with loved ones, or just relaxing alone.

- Learning and Growth against Perfection: Detaching from results also relieves you of the strain of perfection. Instead of worrying about whether your efforts will be successful or unsuccessful, concentrate on what you're learning along the route. This transition from perfectionism to development is freeing, encouraging constant progress over fear of failure.

Developing Self-Trust: The Ultimate Freedom

One of the most major changes that results from letting go is a greater sense of self-trust. As you let go of the need for external validation and control, you start to believe in yourself—your talents, intuition, and ability to overcome life's obstacles.

- Trusting Your Inner Guidance: When you let go of the desire for external acceptance or reinforcement, you begin to depend more on your inner direction. You learn to trust your instincts, make choices that are consistent with your principles, and follow pathways that reflect your actual desires. This inner trust serves as your compass, directing you toward a life that is real and meaningful.

- Embracing Your Resilience: Letting go also allows you to recognize your resilience. By accepting ambiguity, setbacks, and even failure without attempting to control the result, you learn that you have the power to deal with anything life throws at you. This self-reliance promotes a feeling of independence by ensuring that your pleasure and fulfillment are not reliant on external events.

Practical Steps to Living the Freedom Formula

Integrating the Freedom Formula into your daily routine needs practice, attention, and patience. Here are some practical actions to assist you to begin living by this great philosophy:

1. Identify Areas of Control: Consider the areas in your life where you are holding on too strongly. Are you attempting to manage a relationship, a professional result, or how others see you? Awareness is the first step towards letting go.

2. Practice Acceptance: Start by practicing acceptance in simple ways. Accept that you have little influence over how people act, that results may not always match your expectations, and that life will

be full of surprises. Acceptance does not imply giving up; rather, it implies making peace with what is beyond your control.

3. Set Boundaries: Letting go does not imply being passive or allowing people to disregard your needs. Set appropriate limits that preserve your well-being while also enjoying the freedom that comes with relinquishing control over others' behavior.

4. Focus on Process: Whether you're pursuing a goal or navigating a relationship, shift your emphasis from the result to the journey. Find delight in the tiny moments, appreciate incremental progress, and have faith that the process will unfold as it should.

5. Cultivate Self-Trust: Create a solid foundation for self-trust by making choices based on your instincts and ideals. The more you believe in yourself, the less you'll need external approval or control over results to feel safe.

6. Let go of perfectionism: Accept errors and setbacks as chances for development. Giving up the drive for perfection allows you to take chances, learn, and grow without fear of failure.

The Freedom Formula teaches us that genuine pleasure does not result from controlling every element of our lives. Instead, it comes from letting go of the urge for control, accepting unpredictability, and believing in our ability to handle whatever life throws at us. When we let go, we allow ourselves to experience more peace, joy, and fulfillment. We stop spending energy attempting to alter others or foresee the future and instead concentrate on what is genuinely important—living completely and truthfully in the present moment.

As you continue on your path, remember that letting go is a process, not a destination. It demands patience, self-compassion, and a willingness to accept life's uncertainty. However, with each step, you will find a deep feeling of freedom and pleasure that can only be achieved by adhering to the Freedom Formula.

Finally, the best gift you can offer yourself is the freedom to accept what you cannot change and the bravery to live a life that is authentic to you.

www.ingramcontent.com/pod-product-compliance
Lightning Source LLC
Chambersburg PA
CBHW071519220526
45472CB00003B/1073